100

THINGS TO DO IN THE
TWIN CITIES
BEFORE YOU
DIE

100

THINGS TO DO IN THE
TWIN CITIES
BEFORE YOU
DIE

TOM WEBER

Reedy Press
PO Box 5131
St. Louis, MO 63139, USA
www.reedypress.com

Library of Congress Control Number: 2015930929

ISBN: 9781935806981

Design by Jill Halpin

Printed in the United States of America
16 17 18 19   5 4 3

Please note that websites, phone numbers, addresses, and company names are subject to change or cancellation. We did our best to relay the most accurate information available, but due to circumstances beyond our control, please do not hold us liable for misinformation. When exploring new destinations, please do your homework before you go.

DEDICATION

To Kenza, my treasure.

• •

CONTENTS

x

• •

PREFACE

It's awfully nice that you opened this book; that certainly wasn't necessary. I figured you were too busy, but now that you're here, I won't take much of your time. It's just that there are so many gosh darn nice things to see around the Twin Cities that someone should have a list of them in book form, but I didn't really want to pressure you or anything.

We Minnesotans are known as a humble, nice, and largely above average lot who don't care to toot our horn, thank you very much, because the neighbors might be trying to sleep. One of the many jokes about life here in the Land of ten thousand Lakes is that we actually have closer to fifteen thousand lakes but don't want to brag. However, we might have gone a little overboard with humility. The mayor of Minneapolis thought we were being too modest, and she declared an entire week for bragging in 2014. Seven whole days!

And so it is with that absence of trumpeting that I welcome you to my own contribution to Reedy Press's series of 100 things to do in various cities before you die. And while everyone wishes you a long life, good health, and many years to complete your bucket list, there really are some things you should consider here in the Twin Cities to get the full effect of the Minnesota lifestyle.

People in other parts of the country shudder—or maybe

shiver—at the thought of our sometimes fierce and long winters. The only way around it is through it; embracing winter will be duly noted in this list. And the rest of the year is so pleasant and near perfect that it's possible our humility is really a conspiracy to keep it all a secret.

But the secret's out. So if you're visiting, recently moved here, or are a lifer ready to make sure you're well stocked in the "to-do" area of life, I'm happy to present this *100 Things to Do in the Twin Cities Before You Die*. And gosh, it's okay if you only get to twenty or thirty. We're just pleased you're still reading.

Tom Weber

ACKNOWLEDGMENTS

My thanks to Josh Stevens and Reedy Press for the opportunity to write this book; to Amanda Doyle, author of *100 Things to Do in St. Louis Before You Die*, who got me started on this path; to Kim for the helpful edits; and to all my friends who offered ideas on entries for the top 100. And always, to Kenza.

100
THINGS TO DO IN THE
TWIN CITIES
BEFORE YOU
DIE

FOOD AND DRINK

THE ULTIMATE
PATIO RELAXATION

Minnesotans hate to waste a good summer night, knowing winter is always nigh, and there are few better ways to spend such an evening than dining and drinking outside. Many Twin Cities restaurants offer al fresco seating, but few can match the beauty of WA Frost's in the Cathedral Hill neighborhood of St. Paul. Frost's main restaurant occupies most of the first floor of an historic building (check out the awesome basement lounge). The patio is perfected with a subtle but important decoration: trees. They were never cut down, and the patio appears to have been built around them, leaving an ideal canopy to your night and a great place from which to hang lights. You can't help but relax and have a quiet evening with friends on Frost's patio. Consider reservations on busy nights, but waiting for a table isn't the worst thing either.

WA Frost's, 374 Selby Ave., St. Paul
651-224-5715, www.wafrost.com

ENTER THE JUICY
OR JUCY LUCY COMPETITION

A truly Minnesotan thing to eat is the Juicy, or Jucy Lucy—a hamburger with cheese melted inside the patty. Many good people have burned their tongues by biting into a Lucy for the first time as the piping hot cheese squirted into their mouths. But once you've mastered how to eat it (less is more with those first bites), you'll never think of regular hamburgers the same.

Two Minneapolis eateries claim to have invented the marvel: Matt's Bar and The 5-8 Club.

Your task: try both. We'll reserve judgment here. Just note this: at Matt's, they spell it "JUCY LUCY" (without the 'i'); 5-8 spells it "JUICY LUCY," so your very spelling might show favoritism.

President Obama ate at Matt's in 2014, but he never made it to 5-8. Was that a presidential endorsement in this battle, or do we consider his opinion not fully informed?

Matt's Bar & Grill, 3500 Cedar Ave., Minneapolis
612-722-7072, www.mattsbar.com

The 5-8 Club, 5800 Cedar Ave. S., Minneapolis
612-823-5858, www.5-8club.com

PRO TIP

Seriously, be careful the first time you bite into this burger.

A STEAK AND AN OLD-FASHIONED
AT THE OLD-FASHIONED MANCINI'S

If you like steak, there's no point in reading any further. Put down this book and head to the St. Paul institution, Mancini's Char House & Lounge. You can't get more meat and potatoes than this place. And you can't get more retro either.

This place drips with character just the way the garlic bread drips with butter. Not much of the decor has been updated since Mancini's debuted in 1948, and we like it that way. When you're done with dinner, head into the large lounge for an old-fashioned and enjoy some karaoke or the musical devotions of the golden band, the Midas Touch, a Mancini's regular for decades.

Come for the steak, stay for the ambiance, and raise your glass to a truly bygone era.

Mancini's, 531 W. 7th St., St. Paul
651-224-7345, www.mancinis.com

HISTORICAL NOTE

Mancini's had, for several decades, a contemporary in the iconic Nye's Polonaise in northeast Minneapolis, another uber-retro restaurant with its own house band called the World's Most Dangerous Polka Band. Nye's closed its doors in 2016.

EAT THE STREET

It's probably best to head to Eat Street without a specific plan in mind; just follow your inspiration. The name is given to a seventeen-block stretch of Nicollet Avenue just south of downtown that includes dozens of restaurants of all varieties. Park your car or bike and just start walking along Nicollet; see how long it takes you before some restaurant you never even noticed before lures you in.

Longstanding traditional spots and newly opened ones are both available. You can sample German, Japanese, Vietnamese, Thai, African, East African, Greek, diner, and bar food—all of it. Check out the list of restaurants and attractions on the city's website, and plan a day! But not too much planning.

Eat Street, Nicollet Ave., Minneapolis
www.minneapolis.org/partners-community/neighborhoods/eat-street

LUNCH
ON THE TWELFTH FLOOR, PLEASE

There are still hints of the big-city, downtown department stores of yore when you head to the twelfth floor of Macy's in downtown Minneapolis (originally the flagship for the Dayton's chain) for lunch at one of two iconic restaurants.

The Oak Grill opened in 1947 (originally as a men's-only club) and has as its main architectural attraction an ornate fireplace that was already a few hundred years old when it was moved in pieces from England and reassembled. It's a dark but intimate room, perfect for a quiet business lunch or as a stopover during a busy day of shopping. And try the chicken pot pie.

Next door is the Skyroom, which by contrast, offers sweeping views of the city through its floor-to-ceiling windows. The Skyroom is best known for its salad bar.

And while you're there, also check out the exhibit that showcases the history of Dayton's and other department store chains that are key chapters in the history of the Midwest.

The Oak Grill, 700 Nicollet Mall, Minneapolis
612-375-2938, www.macysrestaurants.com/oak-grill

Skyroom at Macy's, 700 Nicollet Mall, Minneapolis
612-375-4555

EAT WITH BEARDS
(BEARDS NOT REQUIRED)

The Twin Cities has a wickedly awesome food scene. An impressive cornucopia of most kinds of ethnic foods is available; the locavore movement is robust, and there's even a healthy food truck scene.

But it's not just the quantity of food. Several Twin Cities restaurants have won the prestigious Beard Award in recent years, and several more were among the nominees. The Beards are considered the Academy Awards for restaurants . . . or maybe the Oscars should be considered the Beards for movies.

This to-do item is simple: find a way to eat at most of these award winners and nominees soon. Your palate will thank you.

They include the famed Kramarczuk's, Al's Breakfast (item #8), 112 Eatery, Restaurant Alma, La Belle Vie, Heartland, Manny's Steakhouse, Piccolo, Saffron, the Bachelor Farmer, Tilia, Butcher & The Boar, Salty Tart, Barbette, Lucia's, Sapor Cafe, Marvel Bar, Rustica, Sea Change, D'Amico, and Travail.

Look them up here
www.jamesbeard.org/awards

CHOOSE YOUR OWN
BEER ADVENTURE

Recent years have seen an explosion of local craft breweries and brewpubs, thanks to a 2011 law that allowed brewers to sell their beer on-site.

So many good beers are now being made across the Twin Cities that you would never be able to sample them all in one effort. So be creative: plan a beer trip to visit several breweries, either by geographical area (walkable sections of town with several breweries) or mode of transport (by bike or light rail).

This entry won't do justice to the newness of the beer scene in the Twin Cities. There's so much to explore. The Minnesota Craft Brewers Guild is one organization with an extensive list of who's out there and worth your visit. Drink responsibly!

Minnesota Craft Brewers Guild
www.mncraftbrew.org
MN Beer
www.mnbeer.com

PRO TIP
Day trip idea: Drive to New Ulm, Minnesota
to tour the historic Schell's brewery.

TAKE PART
IN A BREAKFAST DINER RITUAL

There's a counter at Al's Breakfast with fourteen stools. And that's about it (the place is only about ten feet wide). This Dinkytown mainstay near the University of Minnesota campus is your chance to take part in a morning ritual that dates back almost sixty-five years. The diner appears to have been built in what used to be the alley between the two buildings.

Assuming that all the stools are in use when you get there, just stand along the back wall and wait (eavesdropping is allowed). Once seated, try the pancakes or waffles and be ready to move. The good folks at Al's want to make sure parties of two or three can sit together, so you might need to scooch. It's cool. We're all in this together.

Al's Breakfast, 413 14th Ave. SE, Minneapolis
612-331-9991

SAMPLE FOOD
ON A STICK AT THE STATE FAIR—DAILY

It's fitting to end this list with the iconic state fair, also known as the Great Minnesota Get-Together. This item blends two challenges people have: to attend the fair all twelve days of its annual run and to eat a lot of food on a stick. It's the iconic food, something portable and thus on a stick.

Maybe it's bacon on a stick one day, cheesecake the next, a pancake breakfast the third, or tater tot hotdish (item #76) the fourth. You make your own list of what to eat, and there are new offerings every year. Plenty of sticked samples are available to allow for a daily dose if you're game for twelve trips to the fair. Are you? No one will ever doubt your true Minnesotan cred.

Minnesota State Fair Food
www.mnstatefair.org/find/food

MUSIC AND ENTERTAINMENT

PENUMBRA THEATRE

For the scores of theater options that exist in the Twin Cities, make sure one of them is the Penumbra Theatre in St. Paul. Penumbra is one of a handful of professional African-American theaters in the nation that offer full seasons of shows.

While the theatre itself is unassuming—it shares space with a community center next to a park in the Cathedral Hill neighborhood of St. Paul and seats fewer than three hundred people—the cozy settings and stage add a certain intimacy to the important topics the shows are sure to explore. Penumbra wades into any and all issues surrounding race and the African-American experience in the United States and lays it bare on the stage.

Whether it's a series of adaptations of plays by the famed August Wilson, an important look at the life of Nat King Cole, or a captivating look at daily life in black America with a show literally called "Two Old Black Guys Just Sitting Around Talking," no topics are off limits for Penumbra, and you'll appreciate that when you go.

Penumbra Theatre, 270 N. Kent St., St. Paul
651-224-3180, www.penumbratheatre.org

PRO TIP
Head there early enough for dinner. Several restaurants can be found along nearby Selby Avenue that are well within walking distance (including WA Frost's, item #1) to make for a night of dinner and a play.

PLAY SOME
OLD-FASHIONED HOCKEY

For Minnesotan hockey lovers, the idyllic vision of learning to play as a kid on any random patch of ice comes to life every winter with the US Pond Hockey Championships on Lake Nokomis in Minneapolis. With an aim to play hockey the way it's meant to, as organizers proclaim, grown men and women spend a full weekend outside in January playing hockey.

The game is near-Norman Rockwellian. Players must shovel the ice themselves before each game (no Zambonis). Teams of four try to score on goals made of plywood and boards (think of kids using an old crate). There are refs but no checking, slap shots, or even goaltending. If you can flick the puck into that small opening in the box-goal, you deserve the point.

Players of all skill level enter, so consider dusting off your old skates and scraping together a team. Or, just attend.

US Pond Hockey Championships, Lake Nokomis, Minneapolis
www.uspondhockey.com

GET YOUR MOVIE FIX
AT AN ACTUAL MOVIE THEATER

If cable and internet service ever go out in the Twin Cities, you'll be fine. The Twin Cities host several film festivals each year that you should attend. The biggest and best known is the Minneapolis-St. Paul International Film Festival, which lasts most of April and features more than 150 films from dozens of countries. The event simultaneously prides itself on its international flair and a homegrown smattering of movies with Minnesota connections. Most movies are screened at the St. Anthony Main Theatre in northeast Minneapolis.

But film fests don't end there. Also check out the Twin Cities Film Fest (different than the Minneapolis-St. Paul International Film Fest), the Twin Cities Black Film Festival, Twin Cities Arab Film Fest, Twin Cities Jewish Film Festival, the only known Hmong film festival in the world, and the Minneapolis Underground Film Fest to name just a few.

**Minneapolis-St. Paul
International Film Festival**
612-331-7563
www.mspfilm.org

Twin Cities Film Fest
www.twincitiesfilmfest.org

Twin Cities Black Film Festival
www.facebook.com/tcbff.org

Twin Cities Arab Film Fest
www.mizna.org/arabfilmfest

Twin Cities Jewish Film Fest
www.tcjfilmfest.org

Minneapolis Underground Film Festival
www.mplsundergroundfilmfest.com

Qhia Dab Neeg Film Festival
https://filmfreeway.com/festival/
QhiaDabNeegFilmFestival

RIDE THE RAILS
FOR A TWIN (AND SAINT) BILL

Beginning in 2015, baseball fans will be able to use the Green Line light rail to (potentially) see two games in two cities on the same day. The Green Line starts at Target Field in Minneapolis—home of the Minnesota Twins—and ends at Union Depot in St. Paul's Lowertown neighborhood. From the depot, it's just a long walk from the bullpen to the Saint Paul Saints' new minor league ballpark, due to open in 2015.

Your task: check the Twins' and Saints' schedules to find a date when both teams are home and have staggered enough start times (day/night?) to allow you to watch one game, board the train, and then travel to the other park to see the second. This kind of whirlwind Baseball Day already is possible in such cities as Chicago and New York—and now the Twin Cities.

The fun part is that there might be years with no workable dates, making the double bill all the rarer to accomplish and all the more satisfying to achieve. And keep an eye out for comedian Bill Murray at the new Saints' ballpark; he's part owner of the team.

Minnesota Twins, Target Field, 353 N. 5th St., Minneapolis
612-659-3400, www.minnesotatwins.com
St. Paul Saints, CHS Field
651-644-6659, www.saintsbaseball.com
Green Line (light rail transit)
612-373-3333, www.metrotransit.org

● ●

SPEND HALLOWEEN
IN THE HALLOWEEN CAPITAL
OF THE WORLD

The good people of Anoka, Minnesota, take their Halloween seriously. So much so that the north metro suburb has been designated as the Halloween Capital of the World. The World, people!

City fathers first scared up nearly a month of activities back in 1920 as a way to deter kids from pranks! Idle hands, you know. Now, Anoka fills October with events, including dances; bingo; a high school football game called the Pumpkin Bowl; and one of the largest parades in the state, a staple in the community for decades.

Consider running the Gray Ghost 5K Run before the parade, but wear a costume—you'll run faster.

Recognizing the degree to which Anoka takes seriously its Halloween, the U.S. Postal Service in 2016 announced it would issue Halloween-themed stamps for the first time in its history, and it would mark that occasion in Anoka.

Anoka Halloween
www.anokahalloween.com

GO WILD

Two zoos are located in the Twin Cities, each with its own distinct feel and each worth a visit. The Minnesota Zoo is an expansive, state-run menagerie in suburban Apple Valley. St. Paul Como Zoo sits in the heart of Como Park; it's smaller and older and free! Both have added upgrades in recent years, including Russia's Grizzly Coast at Minnesota Zoo and the new Gorilla House at Como.

And don't forget the animals! Lions, tigers, and bears, indeed. And bugs, birds, sea otters, tortoises, flamingoes, and giraffes. The World of Birds show at the Minnesota Zoo is not to be missed, and neither is the storied Sparky the Sea Lion show at Como. The Como Zoo is also adjacent to a beautiful conservatory to appease your need for tropical flowers (especially in the winter). In non-winter months, the Japanese garden is not to be missed.

Minnesota Zoo (admission charged), 13000 Zoo Blvd., Apple Valley
952-431-9200, www.mnzoo.org

Como Zoo (free admission), 1225 Estabrook Dr., St. Paul
651-487-8201, www.comozooconservatory.org

PRO TIP

Go to the Minnesota Zoo in the spring when its Zoo Babies program features the most adorable critters; the zoo's summer concert series is also worth it. And make sure to utilize Como Zoo's April Fool's Hotline next April 1 to trick your friends into calling Mr. Lion or Ms. Ella Fint.

FIRST AVENUE

The history of the robust Twin Cities' music scene will always prominently include the venue First Avenue. Built in a former Greyhound bus station in downtown Minneapolis, First Ave (you'll stick out if you pronounce the entire word "avenue") rose to national prominence with the 1984 release of the cult classic film Purple Rain. The movie stars the late, great Prince, one of Minnesota's favorite sons, and was released about a month after his wildly successful album of the same name.

Many scenes in the movie take place inside First Ave, and nostalgic fans have flocked to the venue ever since. But they've also flocked for the music. First Ave's still very much a working concert venue. So find a show on the schedule and spend an evening in close quarters with your fellow music lovers. Snap a selfie outside along the wall of stars, featuring the names of performers who have graced the First Ave stage.

Upon Prince's untimely death in 2016, fans flocked to the street in front of First Ave to pay respects, along with his home and recording studio in Chanhassen, Paisley Park.

First Avenue, 701 N. 1st Ave., Minneapolis
612-332-1775, www.first-avenue.com

SEE HOW MANY FRINGE SHOWS
YOU CAN PACK IN

Ever wonder if your coworker Gary from HR is also an amazing performer? He might be performing in the Minnesota Fringe Festival, the largest non-juried fringe festival in the nation. An explosion of performing arts, this event showcases over eight hundred performances of more than one hundred fifty hour-long shows, happening over eleven days at various venues across Minneapolis.

It's structurally impossible to see every show, so choose wisely. The fest is slotted by lottery, meaning there's a wide range of talent on deck. Okay, let's stop sugarcoating: some shows are real duds. But many are brilliant! The fun of the Fringe Fest rests largely in picking shows and figuring out how to race from venue to venue to catch the next one. Spend a full Saturday or Sunday immersed in Fringe. And when you find a dud, embrace it. Organizers say the lemons are the shows people most remember.

Minnesota Fringe Festival
612-872-1212, www.fringefestival.org

HAVE A GRAND OLD DAY

Celebrate the start of summer with a quarter million of your best friends. That attendance mark has the organizers of Grand Old Day in St. Paul claiming to be the largest one-day festival in the Midwest. It's such a popular summer kickoff, in fact, they decided to add a second day in 2016.

St. Paul's Grand Avenue is already known as a can't-miss boulevard of restaurants and shops, but for more than forty years, the first Sunday of every June has seen twenty blocks opened to more than food and merchandise vendors along with several stages with live music. Starting in 2016, the festival will open on Saturday.

The event includes a parade down Grand on Sunday morning. Show up for the floats; stay for the food and festivities.

Grand Old Day
www.grandave.com/grand-old-days

HMONG FREEDOM
CELEBRATION

In the Twin Cities, the Fourth of July weekend doesn't just include fireworks and parades. The Hmong Freedom Celebration and Sports Festival has graced St. Paul summers for more than thirty years.

Known also as "J4," this family-friendly, two-day event in Como Park draws upwards of sixty thousand people from across the world.

Minnesota is home to the nation's second-largest population of Hmong-Americans. Hmong music, food, sport, dress, and pageantry are all on display. And the games! Don't miss the huge soccer tournament and watch a few games of kato, a popular sport in Southeast Asia that's also known as sepak takraw. The game resembles volleyball except you can't use your hands. Players often kick the ball over the net with impressive moves.

Hmong Freedom Celebration and Sports Festival
651-221-0069, www.hmongfc.org

SEE THE JUG BANDS
BATTLE

If the weekend after the Super Bowl leaves you in a funk because there's no more football, how about some jug band music?

That same weekend each year is when you can attend (or compete in) the Battle of the Jug Bands.

The self-proclaimed "oldest and longest running jug band get-together in the known universe"—around since the early '80s—added a second day in recent years with the increasing number of bands. Leave your electric guitars behind, please, and head over to the Nomad and the Cabooze, two bars along Cedar Avenue that host the event.

To qualify as a jug band, bands must be equipped with, of course, a jug, but also three other homemade items. These could include a washtub, spoons, a washboard, stovepipe, or a kazoo made of a comb and tissue paper.

Several awards are handed out, but the bands all have their eyes on the Coveted Hollywood Waffle Iron. *You can keep the Lombardi Trophy, football people.*

Battle of the Jug Bands
www.jugbandmpls.weebly.com/

BE AWED
BY THE COWLES CENTER

The Cowles Center in downtown Minneapolis is a one-stop venue for all things dance in the Twin Cities. Ballet, modern dance, interpretive—it's all there on the specially-with-dance-in-mind stage. Attending a show will make you sorry you ever gave up tap when you were a kid, but that's a normal feeling.

While pondering your own dance what-ifs, take a moment to consider the architecture: the building incorporates the Shubert Theater, which was famously (and slowly) moved in its entirety over twelve days down Hennepin Avenue in 1999. Modern meets must-keep in architecture terms.

Cowles Center for Dance and the Performing Arts
528 Hennepin Ave., Minneapolis
612-206-3636, www.thecowlescenter.org

SET NEW STANDARDS
AT THE DAKOTA

It's a cold Minnesota winter night. You dodge snowbanks on Nicollet Mall and duck into the Dakota Jazz Club, where a full menu promises to meet your every nosh-worthy craving. And just as you finish your meal, feeling contented and a little drowsy, out come the performers to give you a smooth set that we swear really does help with digestion.

The Dakota couldn't be a more intimate setting. Check out their website for their extensive list of guests and reserve your seat now.

If you're a fan of jazz, it won't be long before your time in the Twin Cities includes a trip to the Dakota. The same can be said if you're a fan of good food.

Dakota Jazz Club, 1010 Nicollet Mall, Minneapolis
612-331-1010, www.dakotacooks.com

SPEND HALLOWEEN
IN THE WOODS

Consider spending your next Halloween walking through dark woods to an outdoor puppet show that probably includes a few fires. What could possibly go wrong?

For more than twenty years, the group BareBones Productions has performed an outdoor Halloween pageant on the grounds of some Twin Cities park—usually Hidden Falls in St. Paul. The show has grown in popularity, though organizers still consider it a cult favorite.

The point is to use puppetry, drama, fire, and music to take note of the important connection that Halloween (and autumn) have to the end of life (and the seasons). There's even a chance for audience members to call out and remember those who've died. And at the end, enjoy a free feast of food and drink.

Despite the prominent use of fire, regulars will tell you to bring a blanket and a thermos of something warm (exact item is up to you).

It's truly a unique spectacle not to be missed; it usually runs for a few nights leading up to Halloween.

The Annual Halloween Outdoor Puppet Extravaganza
by BareBones Productions
www.barebonespuppets.org/halloween-show

FRANCONIA
SCULPTURE PARK

You could lose hours wandering the twenty-plus acres of art at the Franconia Sculpture Park, not far from Taylors Falls in the St. Croix River Valley.

It's hard to describe the towering, larger-than-life sculptures you'll see here, in part, because there's always something new. The art is quirky and innovative. Some defy explanation; others make you want to write poetry.

Most of the sculptures are hands-on and sometimes climb-on. Get a snack from the concession stand built into a giant lizard, and then walk through the park possibly hearing the sounds nearby of welders and carpenters creating the next installation. If you go to the Franconia Sculpture Park tomorrow, head back in six months to see what's new.

The park is free and open from sunup to sundown every day of the year.

Franconia Sculpture Park, 29836 Saint Croix Trail, Shafer
651-257-6668, www.franconia.org

FREE MUSIC & MOVIES
IN THE PARK

In our Minnesotan effort to never waste a day of warm, summer weather, the Minneapolis Park Board hosts more than two hundred fifty free concerts and movies across the city.

Most of those—more than two hundred—are music held at one of six parks (Bryant Square, Father Hennepin Bluffs, Lake Harriet, Minnehaha Falls, Nicollet Island, and Theodore Wirth). Those and several other parks throughout the city host the more than sixty movie nights (complete with inflatable movie screen). Did we mention it's free?

The music acts range from the up-and-coming to the Grammy-winning (the Minnesota Orchestra has traditionally played a free outdoor concert every summer), and the movies range from cult classics to family favorites to Minnesota made. They start just after sundown.

Oh, and it's free.

Music and Movies in the Parks, Minneapolis Park & Recreation Board
www.minneapolisparks.org/activities__events/music__movies/

SEE BOTH ORCHESTRAS,
INSIDE AND OUT

The Twin Cities is the rare metropolitan area that hosts not one but two major and renowned orchestras. Both the Minnesota Orchestra and St. Paul Chamber Orchestras are Grammy winners, and both have performance spaces that have recently undergone major renovation work.

Orchestra Hall sits along Nicollet Mall in downtown Minneapolis. The Ordway Center for the Performing Arts in downtown St. Paul is a dynamic presence overlooking Rice Park. Check out both new digs, but also look for outdoor events. These have included Minnesota Orchestra shows at the Lake Harriet Bandshell and SPCO shows at Mears Park. A perfect, family-friendly reason to bring a picnic and hear actual world-class music.

Minnesota Orchestra
www.minnesotaorchestra.org

St. Paul Chamber Orchestra
www.thespco.org

MAY DAY PARADE

The May Day Parade is unlike any other parade of the summer. The puppets are a big reason for that, but so is the festive atmosphere you never quite experience anywhere else.

The event started in the mid-1970s as a thank-you gift, of sorts, from In the Heart of the Beast Puppet and Mask Theatre to the south Minneapolis community for its support. It's now a year-round event where artists and volunteers make puppets large and small to tell a loose-knit story around the year's themes. If you don't help out and march in the parade yourself (no motorized vehicles allowed), then at least be in the audience.

Thousands line Bloomington Avenue to see the creative puppets that range from the handheld to the gigantic and from the adorable to sometimes scary.

If puppets aren't your thing, stick around for (or march in) the "Free Speech Section" of the parade—just bring a cause you support and a banner!

The parade ends with a ceremony and festival in Powderhorn Park. Puppets and humanoids unite!

May Day Parade, In the Heart of the Beast Puppet and Mask Theatre
www.hobt.org/mayday/parade/

APPLAUD MINNESOTA'S
BEST AMATEUR TALENT

Performing in a talent show might conjure memories of some fourth grade pageant where it all went wrong, but now you can exorcise those demons with a trip to the amateur talent contest at the Minnesota State Fair, a fixture for more than forty years. These people deserve to be onstage!

Minnesotans from across the state that have won previous shows either at the state fair or at a county fair are there to sing, dance, play instruments, juggle, or do something called pizza acrobatics (an actual thing). It's a wide range on the entertainment spectrum with three categories—PreTeen, Teen, and Open. The best part is knowing the performers are regular joes and janes who might live next door.

Thousands attend each year at the State Fair Grandstand. Cheer on your neighbors, or sign up yourself! We'll cheer you on!

Minnesota State Fair Amateur Talent Contest
www.mnstatefair.org/competition/talent_contest.html

HEAD TO
LAKE WOBEGON, IN ST. PAUL

The public radio show *A Prairie Home Companion* has become synonymous with the Minnesota way of life. As long-time host Garrison Keillor always proclaims during his weekly news update, the fictional town of Lake Wobegon is "where all the women are strong, all the men are good looking, and all the children are above average." Now that's a goal!

But aside from the idyllic and comedic view of Minnesota life, it's fun to go to the historic Fitzgerald Theater in St. Paul some Saturday evening to see the show made in real time. It's completely different from listening on the radio; seeing the performers on stage together is exciting, but you also get to spend your night in one of the Twin Cities' oldest theater buildings.

After more than forty years at the helm, Garrison Keillor stepped down as host in 2016, handing over the reins to mandolinist Chris Thile. Check it out!

A Prairie Home Companion, Fitzgerald Theater, St. Paul
www.prairiehome.org

PRO TIP

Attend the show in late summer that also includes the annual meatloaf supper and street dance afterward.

A NIGHT OF MUSIC
AT THE TURF CLUB

One of the most unique music venues in the Twin Cities is the Turf Club in St. Paul. Billed as the "best remnant of the '40s," the dive bar/hole-in-the-wall/trendy spot has, in recent decades, become a must-go for live music lovers. With a capacity of around three hundred, it makes for an intimate night of music.

Turf now draws an impressive roster of names from the indie rock scene, especially since it was bought (and renovated) in 2013 by First Ave (see item #16). While doing that renovation work, crews discovered a horse-racing-themed mural that's now on display. Other than that, no frills. And while you're there, head downstairs to the jazz spot known as the Clown Lounge, named for its clown-themed light fixtures and artwork that adorns the walls. If you're genuinely scared of clowns, maybe skip this room.

Turf Club, 1601 University Ave. W., St. Paul
651-647-0486, www.turfclub.net

THE SLEDS
JUST ALL FALL APART

Another way to beat winter is to throw yourself down a hill atop flimsy cardboard or so the organizers of the Art Sled Rally in Powderhorn Park believe.

Held on the third Saturday in January, come snow or snow, all are invited to make a sled (and that's a liberal use of the word "sled") with cardboard or any other materials from your home, and run it down on a cordoned-off hill in Powderhorn Park in south Minneapolis. Spoiler alert: very few sleds make it intact. If laughing were a fuel, though, they'd go for days. You don't get any points for actually getting anywhere.

Coordinated by a group of residents in the Powderhorn Park area and artists who go by the name South Sixteenth High Jinks, the real majesty is the art and effort in creating elaborate sleds. Past creations included an aquarium filled with sledders dressed as various sea life; a replica of London's Tower Bridge; and various game recreations, such as Pac Man and Hungry Hippo. You really have to see it in person.

It's a spectacle, and for a few hours, we all forget it's winter.

Art Sled Rally, Powderhorn Park Neighborhood Association
821 E. 35th St., Minneapolis, 612-722-8640, www.artsledrally.com

GO MEDIEVAL
AT THE RENAISSANCE FESTIVAL

Minnesotans have been traveling back to the 1500s for more than forty years now in what has become the largest Renaissance Festival in the country—three hundred thousand people can't be wrong! Based in suburban Shakopee, the fest runs weekends from late August into October. Bring your dog!

It's enough just to see the fashion and jousting, but there's so much more: sixteen stages with live entertainment fit for a king, including the storied Puke & Snot show. Keep an eye out for some of the street acts, like Beefcake & Olive (you might hear them before you see them) and the Royal Court. Hundreds of booths have real craftsmanship on display (and for sale). Plenty of food is available, and consider a sample of the adult beverage mead—wine made with honey instead of grapes that's made on-site.

This is an all-day, family-friendly event that happens rain or shine.

Minnesota Renaissance Festival, 12364 Chestnut Blvd., Shakopee
952-445-7361, www.renaissancefest.com

TRIVIA

*The famed comedy magic
duo Penn & Teller performed
as a pair for the first time in
1975 at the Minnesota
Renaissance Festival.*

FEEL
THE NORTHERN SPARK

It starts at 9 p.m. and goes until sunrise. Northern Spark is an all-night art festival one night a year—outdoors—in mid-June. You can't help but feel giddy and ready for summer with a trip there.

Organizers pick main spots in the Twin Cities to unleash the art gods. Basically, you can't walk five steps that night without running into the next temporary exhibit, whether that's performance, light shows, art on display, or the time that guy built a cardboard house and then set it on fire in the wee hours (true story).

In some ways, Northern Spark is for the lazy art consumer. You will take in so much art in one night that you could argue you're set for the rest of the year. It's an electric and eclectic event not to be missed.

Northern Spark
http://northern.lights.mn/platform_group/northern-spark/

GET YOUR HANDS DIRTY
AT THE CLAY CENTER

One of the big movie hits of 1990 was *Ghost*, which featured a now-famous PG-13 scene with the main characters (Patrick Swayze, swoon!) making out while using a pottery wheel to make ceramics. It's probably just a coincidence that was the same year the Northern Clay Center opened in Minneapolis.

For more than twenty five years, the center has served as both a gallery of the best ceramics works in the Twin Cities and also a classroom for all of us to explore our inner Swayze. Beginners are more than welcome; many levels of classes are offered.

For those of us who swoon at beautifully crafted plates, vases, glasses or decorative works, this is your chance to fire up the kiln and discover your own skills. And if your piece ends up resembling that pencil holder you made in first grade, so be it! We can't all be Beate Kuhn (look her up), but we should all try.

Northern Clay Center
2424 Franklin Avenue East, Minneapolis
612-339-8007 x301, www.northernclaycenter.org

GET INTO
THE CHRISTMAS SPIRIT
AT ST. OLAF

If you need music to get into the Christmas spirit, don't look for those stations playing *Jingle Bells* all day. Instead, head an hour south of the Twin Cities to Northfield for the St. Olaf Christmas Festival. They've only been doing it for, you know, more than a century (since 1912).

More than five hundred student musicians who are in one of five choirs and the St. Olaf orchestra take part. They perform individually and as an impressive mass ensemble. The event gets national acclaim and broadcast, but being there in person is the real treat, especially for the finale, *Beautiful Savior*.

There are only a few performances, in early December, so be ready to snag your seat when tickets go on sale in October.

St. Olaf Christmas Festival, St. Olaf College
1520 St. Olaf Ave., Northfield www.wp.stolaf.edu/christmasfest

PRO TIP
Get there early enough to take a leisurely walk through the campus before heading to the Skoglund Center Auditorium for the performance.

THE BUFFALO DO ROAM

Hey, remember before European settlers arrived and there were probably more bison around than you could count? And then remember when those settlers killed all the bison?

Funny story: It turns out those bison are actually really important contributors to the health of the prairies and native grasses that existed millennia before Minnesota did.

And so we suggest a trip to see a few efforts to bring back the bison. A non-profit called the Belwin Conservancy—which works to conserve and restore land in the east metro and St. Croix Valley—places bison in their prairies to let them be bison and help restore the land (something about rolling around in the dirt is very helpful).

Head out to the observation platform Belwin set up for Joe Q. Public near Afton. The bison are only there during the warm months of the year, but give them a gander. And remember: Sometimes bison just lay around. Don't expect a show. They're just being bison.

Bison Observation Platform, Belwin Conservancy
Intersection of Stagecoach Trail S & Division Street, Afton
651-436-5189, www.belwin.org/bison/

NOTE
If you're up for a road trip, two other places in Minnesota with bison are Minneopa State Park near Mankato and Blue Mounds State Park near Luverne.

CELEBRATE
CINCO DE MAYO

Head to the west side of St. Paul for the annual Cinco de Mayo Celebration, a one-day, family-friendly event. In addition to a parade along Cesar Chavez Street and live music, you should consider entering jalapeno-eating contests (go for it). Then check out the impressive cars in the low-rider car show, a one-of-a-kind show that includes low-rider bikes! It's a rain or shine event, and it's free.

Cinco de Mayo West Side Celebration
www.cincodemayosaintpaul.com

SPORTS AND RECREATION

DITCH THE CAR

Minneapolis and St. Paul often top (or nearly top) rankings for bike-friendliest cities in the country. Just about any activity in this book can be reached by bike. In addition to miles of urban routes, most lakes and rivers (including the mighty Mississippi) are lined with paths, and getting anywhere is quite possible on a bike—even in the winter when the most hardy souls use fat tires.

If you don't have a bike, rent one. The Twin Cities is among the ever-growing number of metros with a bike rental program (ours is called Nice Ride MN). With just a little practice, you'll find it possible to fill an entire weekend with outings you can get to on two wheels. Don't forget your helmet!

Nice Ride MN
www.niceridemn.org

LUMINATE
YOUR WINTER

Minnesota winters can be famously harsh, which is what makes the Luminary Loppet one of those breathtaking experiences that make you *feel* Minnesotan. It's a short ski jaunt—at night—across one of the Twin Cities' most scenic lakes—Lake of the Isles. The groomed ski path is lined with thousands of luminaries—candles inside little vases made of ice—and a host of "rest stops" for snacks and entertainment (including fire dancers).There are no electric lights on the lake—just the glow of thousands of candles to guide you as you blend your true Minnesotan desire to walk or ski on frozen lakes (perfectly normal in these parts) with that most primal need to interact with neighbors when many retreat to the solitary comfort of heated homes.

You can't help but feel calm, at peace, and happy at this very family-friendly event. No skis? No problem. You're simply asked to walk (or snowshoe) alongside the groomed ski paths.

If you want a quintessential "Minnesota experience," sign up early for next winter's Luminary Loppet.

Luminary Loppet, Lake of the Isles, Minneapolis
612-604-5330, www.loppet.org/luminary-loppet.

NOTE
The Luminary Loppet is one of several events held during a weekend of ski racing activities that range from supercompetitive to not-at-all-competitive (like the luminary), so make sure you're signing up for the right event online.

GUSH OVER
THE FALLS

There's something magical about a waterfall in the center of a major metropolitan area. Minnehaha Falls drops water fifty-three feet at a point inside one of Minneapolis's oldest city parks. Hundreds of thousands of annual visitors (and at least two sitting presidents) have taken in the awesome sight and then maybe grabbed a bite at the nearby restaurant Sea Salt.

The falls rarely disappoint. They slow to a trickle during droughts (a placard near the falls reveals that when President Lyndon Johnson visited in 1964, fire hydrants were opened to "create" a falls). But there's usually a nice, steady flow to whisk you into a moment of urban meditation.

And you needn't wait for summer: the sight of the frozen falls in winter, if not chilly, is an impressive sight for which smartphone cameras were invented.

4801 S. Minnehaha Park Dr., Minneapolis
612-230-6400, www.minneapolisparks.org/parks__destinations/parks__
lakes/minnehaha_regional_park/

PRO TIP

*Walk along Minnehaha Creek after
the falls for that last mile before it empties into
the Mississippi River. The creek there is shallow
and popular for fish-seeking birds, such as the
great blue heron. The hiking paths can flood and
be slippery when the water levels rise, so take note.
But if the paths are dry, walk all the way to the
Mississippi and add another mark to your
Minnesota Experiences
punch card.*

TOUR BOTH CITIES
BY BIKE ON CONSECUTIVE WEEKENDS

For a comprehensive view of both Minneapolis and St. Paul by bike, sign up for the Minneapolis Bike Tour and the St. Paul Classic Bike Tour. They each offer loop courses between fifteen and forty-five miles, and they're usually planned on consecutive weekends. So why not try *both* next year? The events include live bands, rest stops, and technical support if you get a flat.

Several segments of each event are also along closed or partially closed roads, giving you unique views of the cities often only seen by car. Thousands of your neighbors take part in this family-friendly event; join them!

Minneapolis Bike Tour
www.minneapolisbiketour.com

St. Paul Classic Bike Tour
www.bikeclassic.org

PRACTICE
YOUR TRIPLE AXEL

Both Twin Cities' downtowns invite you to explore your inner figure skater with wintertime rinks open to ice dancers of all ages and skill levels. In Minneapolis, head to The Depot, a former train depot building, that also houses hotels and restaurants. In St. Paul, head to WinterSkate, an ice rink erected each winter next to the Landmark Center.

Both places have skate rentals and offer great views of each downtown, but here's the big difference: the Depot rink is indoors; WinterSkate is outdoors. The Depot also has an admission fee in addition to rental costs, whereas WinterSkate only charges for rentals. Pick your preference! If you go in the evening, several restaurants are near each rink for you to make an evening out of it.

Lace up and invigorate your winter with a few laps on the ice.

The Depot Ice Rink, 225 3rd Ave. S., Minneapolis
612-339-2253, www.thedepotminneapolis.com/ice-rink.php

WinterSkate, 75 5th St., St. Paul
612-749-0435, www.wellsfargowinterskate.com

KAYAK THE ST. CROIX

Three major rivers traverse the Twin Cities—the Mississippi, the Minnesota, and the St. Croix. The Mississippi gets most of the glory, but the St. Croix deserves some love. It's a stunning tributary that starts in Wisconsin and spends much of its life as the Minnesota-Wisconsin border. As a National Scenic Riverway, the St. Croix enjoys protections that limit motor boats and jet skis in many places. That leaves a river with stunning natural views and the serenity with which to enjoy them. You'll forget how close you are to a major metropolitan area when you rent a kayak or canoe and amble down the river without a care in the world.

Two popular spots to rent canoes are at Interstate State Park at Taylors Falls, Minnesota, and Wild River State Park near Hinckley, Minnesota. Bring some food for a picnic; several places are available along the way to stop and watch the river. A swim can be refreshing, but be careful of the current, especially if it's been a rainy season and water levels are higher.

Interstate State Park (MN)
Milltown Road, Taylors Falls, MN
www.dnr.state.mn.us/state_parks/interstate/index.html

Taylors Falls Rentals, via Wild Mountain
651-465-6315
www.wildmountain.com/taylors-falls-canoe-kayak-rental

Wild River State Park
39797 Park Trail, Center City, MN
www.dnr.state.mn.us/state_parks/wild_river/index.html

Wild River Rentals, via Eric's Canoe Rental
651-270-1561
www.ericscanoerental.com/index.html

REVIVE
YOUR MINI GOLF GAME

If your mini golf game has grown stale—have the windmill holes started to look the same?—then head over to the Walker Art Center next summer for Artist-Designed Mini Golf. The Walker enlists local artists each year to design holes along the course, leaving them free to express their art. The only requirement seems to be a cup for the ball to drop into.

Ever want to putt under a cadre of suspended soda bottles? Or through a graveyard? Or around some gnomes? Those are some layouts of past courses, but the holes change every year, so keep this item on your perennial to-do list.

Walker on the Green: Artist-Designed Mini-Golf
1750 Hennepin Ave., Minneapolis
612-375-7600, www.walkerart.org

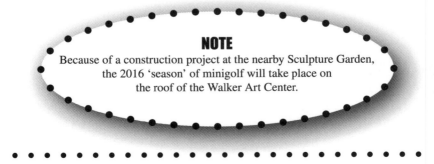

NOTE
Because of a construction project at the nearby Sculpture Garden, the 2016 'season' of minigolf will take place on the roof of the Walker Art Center.

SCREAM YOUR HEAD OFF
AT VALLEYFAIR

This would be a fantastic time for you to get over your fear of roller coasters. Some of the rides at Valleyfair in suburban Shakopee have perfected that feeling of your gut falling away from your shoulders. The Corkscrew and Wild Thing are popular rides, and the Power Tower offers a lovely view from two hundred seventy-five feet above the Twin Cities' suburbs—for about two seconds—before plunging you back to earth.

But for many, it's the High Roller—Valleyfair's classic wooden roller coaster, that debuted in 1976 along with the rest of the amusement park. The oldies really are the goodies.

Also head over to the Soak City waterpark and cool off on a hot summer day.

Valleyfair, 1 Valleyfair Dr., Shakopee
(952) 445-7600, www.valleyfair.com

APPRECIATE
THE RIVER

The histories of Minneapolis and St. Paul are nothing without rivers. The Mississippi begins as a trickle in Lake Itasca State Park in northern Minnesota (worth the trip) and flows through its first major metropolitan area at Minneapolis-St. Paul.

But for all the 2,320 miles of river from Minnesota to the Gulf of Mexico, the Twin Cities is the only section of river that's also a national park, the seventy-two-mile Mississippi National River and Recreation Area.

Head to the park's headquarters in St. Paul (in the Science Museum, item #89) to learn about all the activities to be had on this specially designated stretch.

Look for hidden hikes along the river too. We suggest Hidden Falls Regional Park, with breathtaking views of the river, bird-watching, and some serious thinkin' time.

Mississippi National River and Recreation Area
Visitors Center: 120 W. Kellogg Blvd., St. Paul
651-290-4160, www.nps.gov/miss/index.htm

CHEER
ON THE RUNNERS

If you want to run a marathon, you absolutely should. It's a great accomplishment. But if you're not all that keen to learn where your body most easily chafes, consider at least watching the Twin Cities Marathon.

Held on the first Sunday in October, spectators and runners will know they've treated the weather gods well if they awake to a brisk morning that becomes a beautiful fall day. The course of the marathon showcases the Twin Cities—starting in downtown Minneapolis, weaving along lakes, creeks, and rivers and over to St. Paul up its iconic Summit Avenue with a triumphant finish line at the State Capitol (item #64).

As a spectator, any spot along this course is a great place to set down a lawn chair and marvel at the work it takes to train for a marathon. Runners genuinely appreciate the cheering masses that motivate them to the end. You won't get a medal for cheering, but you'll have done your part.

Twin Cities Marathon
651-289-7700, www.tcmevents.org

LAWN BOWLING
AT BRIT'S

Everything about Brit's Pub in downtown Minneapolis is British, from the ales on tap to the fish 'n chips on the menu, but head upstairs to the rooftop level and take in, or play, a game of lawn bowling. It's an easy enough game for anyone to learn. It resembles Bocce; players roll their bowls, as they're called, closest to the jack.

There are open hours every weekend for any Johnny-come-latelies. Another option is to join a lawn bowling league, but Brit's website proclaims to have a ten-year wait list! Sure, playing a no-stress game with your friends while sipping a pint is enticing, but now add in the backdrop of the downtown Minneapolis skyline on a warm summer evening, and you'll understand why this rooftop attraction is a can't-miss.

Brit's Pub Lawn Bowling, 1110 Nicollet Mall, Minneapolis
612-332-3908, www.britspub.com/lawn_bowling/

WALK
ON THE WATER

The idea of walking on a frozen lake might sound haunting and scary . . . at first. But then that hardy, Minnesotan, let's-beat-winter drive takes over. Make sure your time in the Twin Cities includes a walk across a frozen lake.

Yes, it's freezing and usually very windy, but if you're bundled up, there's also something very peaceful about standing in the middle of a lake (especially at night) and feeling a little removed from the rat race. The tongue-in-cheek rule about lake walking is "Never Be the First Person to Walk on a Lake."

Take special care when lakes are first freezing in the winter and thawing in the spring. At the height of winter, though, and at the height of below-freezing temperatures, an ice jaunt will be uneventful.

Consider also the scattering of events during the winter that take place on frozen lakes, such as the Kite Festival on Lake Harriet in Minneapolis (which also has ice fishing demonstrations).

HELP
COUNT THE BIRDS

We're a bird-loving bunch, we Minnesotans. So much so that the local Audubon Society has, since 1905, hosted an annual Christmas Bird Count. Volunteers sit outside for a few hours every December and literally count (and identify) the birds that go by.

This falls under one of those "greater good" categories. Yes, it's largely a volunteer effort, but because it's happened for more than a century, the data have become essential for researchers.

Even though it happens at the height of winter and you don't get paid for your time, the spots usually fill up. Bring your binoculars!

Christmas Bird Count, Minnesota Ornithologists' Union
www.moumn.org

WALK YOURSELF
AROUND THE U

The University of Minnesota, established in 1851, is older than the state of Minnesota and has many fine, old buildings to prove it. Don't let another summer go by without a self-guided walking tour of the campus. The Minneapolis campus sits on both sides of the Mississippi River, and you could easily spend an entire day exploring.

One place to start is Pillsbury Drive, a row of the U's oldest buildings. A stroll starts at the Armory and heads along the impressive Pillsbury Hall, with its stones and arches. Other landmarks along Pillsbury include Nicholson Hall, Eddy Hall, and Burton Hall, along with the underground Williamson Hall, a newer structure built underground. Just off Pillsbury Drive is the glorious Northrop Hall, visible on your walk.

University of Minnesota
www.umn.edu

WANDER SWEDE
HOLLOW

Swede Hollow is not St. Paul's largest park, but its unique layout in a deep ravine begs for a visit. It also has a colorful, if not checkered history.

Home for decades to St. Paul's poorest immigrants, the final residents were evicted and the buildings were burned in the 1950s.

Swede Hollow then became a woodland with a few visible signs of its history in a few corners. Walking and biking paths guide your visit, and you're not too far from the Bruce Vento Nature Sanctuary (item #53), so head there after you've taken in Swede Hollow.

If you're wondering what the huge abandoned-looking, fenced-off factory is at the northern end of the park, that's the former Hamm's Brewery. Flat Earth, a new brewery, is one of the new occupants.

Swede Hollow Park
www.stpaul.gov/facilities.aspx?page=detail&rid=97

BRUCE VENTO NATURE
SANCTUARY

One of the best features of the Twin Cities is a healthy supply of spots that seem far removed but are actually just a few steps from a major city center. One of those is the Bruce Vento Nature Sanctuary, a twenty-seven-acre patch of land just outside the edge of downtown St. Paul that is a true escape.

It's an escape even though you can clearly see the downtown St. Paul skyline, and you can hear trains from the rail yard next door. But the sanctuary is also perfectly situated at the base of a bluff that makes you feel cozily nested. Ducks usually hold court in the ponds on the eastern end of the sanctuary, and several good sittin' rocks are around for one to ponder life. And the abandoned Lowertown Depot building is a sight, though it's likely to be razed in coming years.

Bruce Vento Nature Sanctuary, 4th St. E., St. Paul
651-266-6400, www.lowerphalencreek.org/edresources2.html

BIKE TO STILLWATER
FOR LUNCH

A trip to Stillwater is a must. Nestled along the idyllic St. Croix River, downtown Stillwater is a perfect place to spend the day antiquing, shopping, and eating. But now consider really earning it: grab your bike and ride the twenty-ish mile trip there!

Take the Gateway State Trail, which starts about a mile or so from the State Capitol in St. Paul. A picture-perfect, tree-canopied trail, you'll rue the day you ever thought to drive to Stillwater! Near Highway 96, pick up the Brown's Creek State Trail for the final six miles into Stillwater.

If a forty-mile bike round-trip is daunting, make this your summer challenge. Start training in the spring, and plan for your trip in early fall!

Gateway State Trail
www.dnr.state.mn.us/state_trails/gateway/index.html

Brown's Creek State Trail
www.dnr.state.mn.us/state_trails/browns_creek/index.html

Visit Stillwater
www.discoverstillwater.com

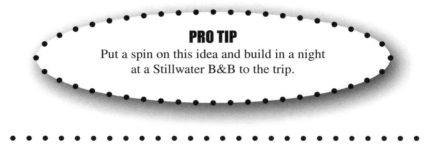

PRO TIP
Put a spin on this idea and build in a night
at a Stillwater B&B to the trip.

IF YOU CAN'T ARBORETUM
JOIN 'EM

The trees are your friends, as you'll learn with a trip to suburban Chanhassen to the University of Minnesota Landscape Arboretum. More than eleven hundred acres of lush trees and plants await you year-round. Check out the twenty-eight gardens, including the rose, Japanese, and waterfall gardens, and take the bog boardwalk through a wetland. The Arboretum is an easy place to get lost in with the wandering trails (wheelchair access is limited in some areas); you'll come home with plenty of garden tips. You can also venture by car though the main road closes to cars in winter.

The cafeteria is good for lunch; lots of windows look out on the landscape.

Minnesota Landscape Arboretum, 3675 Arboretum Dr., Chaska
952-443-1400, www.arboretum.umn.edu

PRO TIP
Come back in the winter to use sixteen miles
of cross-country ski trails.

PADDLE A CHAIN
OF LAKES

Along the northeast shoreline of Lake Calhoun in Minneapolis, you should rent a kayak or canoe or paddleboard or boat and course your way through three of the famed Chain of Lakes. Head immediately to the canal under Lake Street that connects Calhoun to Lake of the Isles (home of the Luminary Loppet, item #39). Take in the views of the beautiful houses as you keep along the west edge of the lake. Then take the canal under Lake of the Isles Parkway that connects to Cedar Lake. That canal will be an idyllic paddle along backyards. On Cedar Lake, turn right and head over to Hidden Beach for a swim. Then head back for lunch at the Tin Fish on Lake Calhoun.

Lake Calhoun Rental, via Wheel Fun Rentals
3000 Calhoun Parkway East, Minneapolis
612-823-5765, www.wheelfunrentals.com

Tin Fish, 3000 Calhoun Parkway East, Minneapolis
612-823-5840, www.tinfishmpls.com

FLOAT ALONG
MINNEHAHA CREEK

Another watercraft must is tubing Minnehaha Creek. There are no rental places along the creek, though, so you'll have to use your imagination to procure an inner tube or rent a kayak or canoe from a local outfitter. Minnehaha Creek runs twenty-two miles from Lake Minnetonka (item #69) to the Minnehaha Falls (item #40). Pick a segment along that stretch to lazily let the currents take you downstream. The creek runs through backyards in Edina but mostly parkland in Minneapolis—a little bit for everyone! Bring a picnic and find a spot to have lunch along the way.

Minnehaha Creek Watershed District
www.minnehahacreek.org

PRO TIP
This can be a tricky outing to plan if the creek levels are too high or too low. Keep an eye on notices from the Minnehaha Creek Watershed District.

CRASHED ICE

Nothing like a truly extreme sport to heat up winter, and we can confirm the Red Bull Crashed Ice event in St. Paul has both crashing and ice.

It's become a popular draw of several thousands of people on cold nights in January to watch competitors skate down a twisting course of ice. The track is temporary, built in the shadow of the iconic Cathedral of St. Paul. The sport, officially called ice cross downhill racing, combines hockey, downhill skiing, and the luge.

You can try out (and sign a lot of waiver forms) if you want, or you can all but eliminate your risk of a broken leg by just watching in person. Dress warmly and marvel at the extremes sports have attained.

Red Bull Crashed Ice, Selby & John Ireland Blvd., St. Paul
www.redbull.com/us/en/events/1331691303521/crashed-ice-saint-paul

LEARN TO CURL
AT THE ST. PAUL CURLING CLUB

The winter sport of curling seems to captivate the nation every four years at the Olympics (the entire 2014 USA men's team was from Minnesota). But don't just wonder what those brooms are for—learn to sweep on the ice yourself at the St. Paul Curling Club, the oldest curling club in Minnesota.

Players throw stones or rocks down sheets of ice, trying to get closest to the house—a circular target on the ice. The game is all finesse, and the brooms play a big role in how the rocks turn or slow down or don't slow down. Take in a few games at the club, and then inquire about joining a league and try your hand. And don't be surprised to see some Olympians playing on the sheet next to you. Good curling!

St. Paul Curling Club, 470 Selby Ave., St. Paul
651-224-7408, www.stpaulcurlingclub.org

CULTURE AND
HISTORY

SPAN
THE STONE ARCH BRIDGE

One of the most iconic images of the Twin Cities is the downtown Minneapolis skyline, which features one of the Mississippi River's most unique bridges—the Stone Arch Bridge. Featuring twenty-three arches of stone and built for trains by railroad baron James J. Hill (see item #90) in the 1880s, it opened for pedestrians and bikes only in 1994, offering the best view yet of St. Anthony Falls and the skyline.

It's easy to spend an evening on and around the bridge or an entire weekend! Father's Day weekend is now set aside for the Stone Arch Festival, which features art and music on the St. Anthony side of the river, with a perfect view of the bridge.

Stone Arch Bridge, 1 Portland Ave., downtown Minneapolis
www.minneapolisparks.org
www.nps.gov/miss/planyourvisit/stonarch.htm

FIND THE END
OF THE ENDLESS BRIDGE

As noted in item #60, the downtown Minneapolis skyline is a must. But where's the best vantage point? We suggest the Guthrie Theater's Endless Bridge. A cantilevered lobby that extends one hundred seventy-eight feet from the building face, the endless bridge is a dramatic and exquisite spot.

Most of the bridge is indoors, with windows the designer framed to force your view on certain landmarks, according to Guthrie's website. The final part of the bridge is outdoors, giving you that panoramic river view.

The Guthrie theater building, perched along the riverfront, actually houses three theaters that are open year-round to performances, but you don't need a show ticket to still walk inside and take the escalator to the endless bridge. The attraction acts almost as a fourth theater, with the Minneapolis riverfront as the stage. Plan to spend considerable time thinking and taking pictures here.

Endless Bridge, Guthrie Theater, 818 S. 2nd St., Minneapolis
612-377-2224, www.guthrietheater.org

RUIN A DAY
AT MILL CITY MUSEUM

We know we're asking a lot here, but trust us when we say one of your best family outings will be a museum dedicated to flour that includes an elevator as a main highlight. Stay with us: modern Minneapolis history is forever tied to the Mississippi River, whose sheer force at St. Anthony Falls was harnessed to provide water for a burgeoning flour industry that would shape the nascent city's future.

The Washburn-Crosby Company (later known as a little company called General Mills) built its first mills along the river in the 1880s. After a fatal explosion that leveled several mills in 1878, a new Washburn A Mill was opened in 1880 and produced the famed Gold Medal Flour until 1965. That building, left vacant for decades, was gutted by a massive fire in 1991.

But making lemonade out of lemons, the Mill City Museum was built inside the burned ruins. Marvel at the architecture, but don't miss the Flour Tower, a tricked-up elevator ride that offers a vertical view (with recreated machinery) of how the mill's floors once looked. And don't miss the observation deck atop the building, with stunning views of the falls. On your way out, grab free samples of whatever's being made in the Baking Lab. Exhibits also show the history of iconic brands like Pillsbury (and its famed doughboy mascot, Poppin' Fresh), Wheaties, and Bisquick.

Mill City Museum, 704 S. 2nd St., Minneapolis
612-341-7555, www.millcitymusuem.org

PRO TIP

Head there during the summer on a day when the museum is hosting a concert in its courtyard—the best place to see the mill's ruins—and enjoy a soundtrack to your visit.

DO FARM CHORES
AT THE KELLEY FARM

Sure, your own laundry sits undone, but that shouldn't stop you from heading to the Oliver H. Kelley Farm to help them with their chores!

This is one of those places that sneak in good old-fashioned learning by covering it with fun. Located in suburban Elk River on land once owned by Oliver H. Kelley, visitors can see firsthand a hint of what it was like to live on a farm in the 1850s, when this part of Minnesota was still very much frontier land.

Kelley is best known as founder of the national farming organization known as the Grange. It's a working farm; staff wear period clothing and invite visitors to help with gardening, field chores, cooking, and other tasks. You can go from plowing a field to making molasses to learning the history of agriculture in a few hours. Parents: the farm is a popular school field trip, so you might end up being taught by your own children when you go.

And don't forget the farm animals! The oxen seem to be the big draw for kids. As one former employee noted, it's "crazy how throwing in an ox makes kids beg to do chores." We do not recommend getting an ox as a motivator for your own home chores. The farm is open from Memorial Day to Labor Day.

Oliver H. Kelley Farm, 15788 Kelley Farm Road, Elk River, MN 55330
763-441-6896, www.sites.mnhs.org/historic-sites/oliver-h-kelley-farm

TOUR
THE STATE CAPITOL

One of Minnesota's architectural marvels is its State Capitol. Famed architect Cass Gilbert designed some of the nation's first skyscrapers and the US Supreme Court building in Washington, D.C., but his work on the Minnesota Capitol arguably put him on the map nationally.

It opened in 1905 as the state's third capitol building. The best view is from the rotunda looking up into the massive and breathtaking dome (one of the largest self-supporting marble domes in the world). You should also stand on the front steps and look out on the extensive capitol grounds, along with perfect views of downtown St. Paul and the impressive Cathedral of St. Paul. If you come during the legislative session, you're sure to see a rally trying to raise attention for a cause. Join a cause! This entry has an asterisk: at the time of this writing, a massive restoration is under way. Still, the building is impressive enough to keep in this book. Stay patient and definitely visit after restoration work is done, which is scheduled for 2017.

Minnesota State Capitol, 75 Rev. Dr. Martin Luther King Jr. Blvd., St. Paul
651-296-2881, www.sites.mnhs.org/historic-sites/minnesota-state-capitol

GO ON A TREASURE HUNT
... REALLY

Another way to beat winter is to crawl through it . . . while looking for the St. Paul Pioneer Press Medallion. The treasure hunt dates back to the 1950s and coincides with the St. Paul Winter Carnival. St. Paul's daily newspaper, the *Pioneer Press*, posts clues once a day for up to twelve days for where to find the medallion.

It's buried somewhere, usually a park, in Ramsey County. But it's more complicated than that. The medallion is often buried very well, including being encased in ice, resting inside the pocket of a pair of jeans, or taped to a food canister and buried in snow. It's not uncommon to hear about people taking off work to search, but they have a great motivation: the reward for finding the medallion is up to $10,000. Vacation day, anyone?

St. Paul Pioneer Press Treasure Hunt
www.twincities.com/treasurehunt

List of previous medallion locations:
www.twincities.com/treasurehunt/ci_22395861/
pioneer-press-treasure-hunt-medallion-locations

SEE LIFE-SIZED PRINCESSES
CARVED IN BUTTER

Head to the Dairy Building at the Minnesota State Fair and behold the wonders of the butter princesses. Each year the Midwest Dairy Association holds the pageant known as "Princess Kay of the Milky Way." Princess Kay and her court, who all hail from dairy families, each get their likeness carved into ninety pounds of butter.

They and the butter sculptor sit in a small rotating refrigerated booth for nearly six hours in the Dairy Building while we gawk at the wonder of butter art.

Midwest Dairy Association, Dairy Building
Minnesota State Fair, Corner of Judson & Underwood
www.midwestdairy.com/0t245p272/princess-kay-of-the-milky-way/

EXORCISE YOUR FEAR OF HEIGHTS
AT THE STATE FAIR

You don't have to live in Minnesota long to learn that the state fair in Falcon Heights is iconic, with plenty of traditions, both food and attractions. But don't pass up the chance to see the fairgrounds from above.

There are several ways: two sky rides move riders by cable overhead and across much of the fairgrounds. Sit back and enjoy this ten-minute ride and take in all the views.

There's also the Space Tower, an observation tower that lifts a room of passengers three hundred thirty feet into the air. The tower also rotates, so you'll gain a three hundred sixty-degree view!

And the fire tower at the DNR booth is modeled after those in the woods that rangers use to monitor the landscape. This is a free climb of eighty-four steps (take note if you're not a climber) to view the fair from sixty-five feet up.

Anyone can eat food on a stick while firmly planted on the ground. Why not take to the air?

Minnesota State Fair
www.mnstatefair.org

RIDE HISTORIC
STREETCARS

Like many cities, the Twin Cities had an extensive streetcar network in the early twentieth century that fizzled as cars became ever more en vogue. Fortunately, a stretch of track remains between Lakes Harriet and Calhoun in Minneapolis, where you can enjoy the clang clang of the trolleys through a scenic wooded area.

Some trolleys date back more than one hundred years, and the Minnesota Streetcar Museum operates them during warm weather months. All streetcar operators are serious train buffs who volunteer their time (and have proper training as streetcar drivers). The ride is just a few minutes, but if you're lucky, the memories last forever.

Hours are seasonal and trips canceled when it rains to protect the restored streetcars. This a super family-friendly attraction, but the old streetcars have limited capacity for people with disabilities, so contact them ahead of time with questions.

Como-Harriet Streetcar
www.trolleyride.org

PRO TIP
The Minnesota Streetcar Museum also operates a similar line in Excelsior, Minnesota, on the banks of Lake Minnetonka. Ride both lines and compare!

RIDE HISTORIC STREETCARS
... ON THE WATER

Once you tackle item #68, do the same thing on the waters of one of Minnesota's best-known lakes! Take a cruise (weekends and holidays during warm weather months) of Lake Minnetonka on a "streetcar boat" fashioned to look like old streetcars and originally used to transport residents across the lake. After that era, the boats were scuttled.

But one of them, now called Steamboat Minnehaha, was dredged from the bottom of the lake and restored in the 1980s.

In its heyday, Lake Minnetonka (and its amusement park that no longer exists) was the terminus of an oft-traveled streetcar line. The streetcars remain, with one on land in Excelsior and one on water. Climb aboard!

Steamboat Minnehaha
www.steamboatminnehaha.org/tickets.cfm

TRY
LUTEFISK

Every hardy Minnesotan really should try lutefisk at least once. Stemming from the state's deep Scandinavian heritage, lutefisk is a fish entree (often cod) prepared by being soaked in lye and steamed. It's a highly mocked dish because, well, so many people find it disgusting. The general rule is that lutefisk (pronounced LOO-teh-fisk) is only swallowable (never mind tasty) if drenched in butter.

Lutefisk has its defenders, though, and the world's largest lutefisk processor is in Minneapolis! There's something to be said for a staple that remains a staple even when it's unloved. Lutefisk is like Scandinavia's fruit cake, and if Minnesotans don't embrace it, who will?

Several churches, VFWs, and community centers serve lutefisk during fall and holiday season events, so a quick internet search should yield a nearby event. The Annual Lutefisk Dinner at Mount Olivet Lutheran Church in Minneapolis, for example, is usually held the first Friday in December and dates back to 1929. More than twelve hundred pounds of the fish are served; it's not clear how much butter is consumed.

THE NEWBORN ANIMALS
ARE ADORABLE

A key reason the Minnesota State Fair is truly the state's get-together is the livestock shows that bring high schoolers (and their families) from across the state to showcase their prized cows, sheep, goats, poultry, and even llamas. But for those animals in no condition to walk around, head over to the Miracle of Birth center to see farm life's debut.

With veterinarians on hand if needed, visitors can't help but view either a live or taped birth being shown on one of the many monitors throughout the building. Yes, birthing is messy and a healthy cacophony of "ewwws" season the soundtrack of the moment, but your heart will melt with the opportunity to see (and pet) the cleaned-up critters—including baby chicks and sheep!—as they ponder their existence during farmland's version of the debutante ball.

Miracle of Birth Center (During MN State Fair)
www.mnstatefair.org/entertainment/ag_exhibits/chs_mob.html

CHERRY SELFIES
AT THE SCULPTURE GARDEN

One of the Twin Cities' iconic images is a huge sculpture of a spoon holding a cherry, with the downtown Minneapolis skyline in the background. That installation, called "Spoonbridge and Cherry," is the best-known spot inside the Minneapolis Sculpture Garden.

More than forty pieces of public art fill this peaceful eleven-acre garden, which is perfect for strolling and sitting. Once you find the spoon and cherry (which is also a fountain), try trick photography. Stand far enough away to frame a photograph with you in the foreground that gives the appearance of you holding the spoon and eating the cherry. Test your photo skills!

Minneapolis Sculpture Garden, 725 Vineland Pl., Minneapolis
www.walkerart.org/garden/

NOTE
A massive restoration closed the garden in 2016, so be sure to stand in line for its reopening in 2017.

HAVE A JOLLY GOOD TIME
AT THE BRITISH ARROWS

We Minnesotans sure do enjoy the adverts those Brits put on the telly. Our friends across the pond have for nearly forty years bestowed awards called the British Arrows on the best ads in their land, and for nearly thirty years, the Walker Art Center in Minneapolis has hosted screenings of the award winners.

The ads range from the dramatic to the inventive to the tear-jerking and heartwarming to the out loud, make-you-cry-with-laughter ingenious.

The British are coming . . . with their ads . . . and you should be happy about it.

British Arrow Awards at the Walker Art Center
1750 Hennepin Ave., Minneapolis
612-375-7600, www.walkerart.org

PRO TIP
Buy tickets early; screenings often sell out.

HAVE DRINKS
ATOP THE FOSHAY

The Foshay tower is easy to spot; it's the one with the big word "FOSHAY" across the top. It's staggering to imagine that, for a time, Foshay was the tallest building west of the Mississippi River.

It was completed in 1929, just a few months before its namesake, Wilbur Foshay, lost everything in the stock market crash.

The architectural marvel reopened as a hotel in 2008. Head to the Prohibition Bar on the twenty-seventh floor for a cocktail and take in the panoramic views amidst impressive woodwork. A museum and observation deck are on the thirtieth floor. That deck is not wheelchair accessible and not always open during winter, so call ahead.

Foshay Museum & Observation Deck, 821 Marquette Ave., Minneapolis
612-215-3783, www.foshaymuseum.com/home.html

Prohibition Bar
612-215-3700, www.wminneapolishotel.com/prohibition-bar

SEE JESSE JAMES
IN NORTHFIELD

Drive about an hour south of the Twin Cities to the charming town of Northfield. Part of the charm is its quaint downtown of shops and restaurants and being home to not one but two small liberal arts colleges, St. Olaf and Carleton. The town's motto is "Cows, Colleges & Contentment."

Consider also a summer trip to relive the history of Jesse James. The James/Younger gang's ill-fated robbery of the Northfield's First National Bank in 1876 is reenacted every summer at the Defeat of Jesse James Days, complete with raid, shootout, and getaway.

Defeat of Jesse James Days, Downtown Northfield, www.djjd.org

WHIP UP
A HOTDISH

We Minnesotans have a funny way of pronouncing the word casserole. We say "hotdish." Now, a purest will claim there's a difference between a casserole and a hotdish, but we're not sure we could.

So, in the spirit of being a true Minnesotan, we invite you to try your hand at creating the quintessential of all hot dishes, the tater tot hot dish. Your most basic ingredients will be cream of mushroom soup, tater tots, and ground beef. Plenty of recipes are to be found online for guidance, but if any ancestors were Minnesotan, your family probably has its own heirloom recipe.

Then, when you've perfected the ultimate Minnesota concoction, see how you stack up against your neighbors by entering that hotdish in a competition. Minnesota's members of Congress have held their own such hotdish-off in recent years, but short of winning your own election, you could always start with Hotdish Revolution, a competition hosted by the Holland Neighborhood Improvement Association in northeast Minneapolis.

It's one thing to have a great hotdish recipe; it's another to have an award to your name.

Hotdish Revolution, Holland Neighborhood Improvement Association
www.facebook.com/HotdishRevolution
www.hnia.org

TOUR
THE GOVERNOR'S MANSION

Horace Hills Irvine was never governor, but the swanky mansion he built (for $57,000) in the 1910s along historic Summit Avenue in St. Paul is today the official Minnesota Governor's Residence. Donated in the 1960s, the fenced-off acre that includes an impressive terrace and garden out back is very much the current governor's home.

And just as you don't want anyone walking through your living room anytime they want, the Governor's Residence is open only occasionally for tours. Keep an eye on the website for dates; the holiday tours are especially popular. That's when the house's seven bedrooms, ten bathrooms, and nine fireplaces are decorated by various designers from across Minnesota.

Minnesota Governor's Residence, 1006 Summit Ave., St. Paul
www.mn.gov/admin/governors-residence/

BEHOLD,
THE DIORAMA!

Dioramas might have been a more popular art form in the early 1900s, but a visit to the Bell Museum of Natural History reveals a stark truth: when done well, they are meticulous marvels of craftsmanship.

The Bell dates back more than one hundred forty years, and behind the scenes its collection of millions of plant and animal specimens are crucial for research. But the museum's public face is dozens of incredible dioramas from the '40s and '50s that showcase Minnesota's rich and diverse wildlife habitat. From the extinct (passenger pigeon) to the thriving (black bears, squirrels, heron, and deer) and the mysteriously disappearing (moose), visitors come face-to-face with Minnesota's menagerie in displays that blend painted backgrounds with taxidermy and other elements to complete the foreground.

Then head to the "Touch and See" room and do just that . . . feel animal hides, antlers, and bones, and see a few live animals also on display, including turtles, tarantulas, and frogs.

There's also a small planetarium there, and stay tuned! Big plans are ahead for a bigger Bell with more space stuff and, of course, the dioramas. That new museum will be located on the University of Minnesota's St. Paul campus and is expected to open in 2018.

The Bell Museum of Natural History, 10 Church St. SE, Minneapolis
(on the University of Minnesota campus)
612-626-9660, www.bellmuseum.org

EXPLORE RUSSIAN ART
IN SOUTH MINNEAPOLIS

At first glance, the Museum of Russian Art seems out of place. It's the only museum in North America dedicated to all forms of Russian art, and it's located in the former Mayflower Congregational Church in south Minneapolis built in the Spanish Colonial Revival style.

So it's a testament to the designers who transformed this building from church to art gallery. The key appears to be a glass-lined mezzanine that allows a second floor of art inside the former main sanctuary space. Here, the ever-changing exhibits will wow you with glances inside Russia during the time of Peter the Great or the czars or the Soviet era or Putin. It's a good place to put away stereotypes you have of the country and its long history and gain a new perspective.

You can also visit the basement gallery and second-floor gift shop, where you can stock up on matryoshka dolls and Russian tea.

The Museum of Russian Art, 5500 Stevens Ave. S., Minneapolis
612-821-9045, www.tmora.org

MODEL RAILROAD
MUSEUM

Why are model railroads so mesmerizing? The cars go by, the miniature gates go up and down, the signals turn on and off, and then it's an hour later. Thus sums up your next trip to the Twin City Model Railroad Museum, which has been transfixing St. Paulites since 1934.

Formerly housed inside Bandana Square, the museum in 2016 moved to a new site on Transfer Road, near a former Amtrak depot. The main attraction is a large and amazingly detailed O-scale model of the Twin Cities, featuring the mills, depots, and rail yards of yore (the Stone Arch Bridge is depicted when it was a train crossing!).

Staffed by a volunteer cadre of train buffs, it's hard to distinguish the bigger kids in this hobby wonderland.

Twin City Model Railroad Museum, 668 Transfer Road, St. Paul
651-647-9628, www.tcmrm.org

NOTE
To see fullsize trains on display, head to the Minnesota Transportation Museum and Jackson Street Roundhouse in St. Paul, or take a road trip to the Lake Superior Railroad Museum in Duluth.

GET LOST
IN THE MINNEAPOLIS INSTITUTE
OF ARTS

There's no good way to describe the enormity of the Minneapolis Institute of Arts (now referred to as "Mia," pronounced "mee-uh"). With its long, sweeping galleries and hallways, it sometimes feels downright Louvre-like. The building itself is also an impressive landmark.

Find artifacts, paintings, photographs, and sculptures spanning six thousand years of cultural history. If you don't like the art in this room, just walk to the next one. There's something for everyone here, from ancient Chinese Buddhist art, a world-renowned Japanese art collection, and an exhibit of Prairie School-style architecture, to the latest work from Minnesota artists, to the annual Art in Bloom show. It's okay to get lost; wear walking shoes. Admission is free (suggested donations accepted at the door), and while most art is hands-off, it's a family-friendly-outing.

Minneapolis Institute of Arts, 2400 3rd Ave. S., Minneapolis
612-870-3000, www.artsmia.org

PRO TIP #1

Several points along the north side of the building have floor-to-ceiling windows that offer perfect views of the downtown Minneapolis skyline.

PRO TIP #2

There's an old Otis elevator installed in 1930 that still functions today. Use it!

PRO TIP #3

After being inside, consider a walk outside on the MIA grounds along with MCAD (Minneapolis College of Art and Design) and Washburn Fair Oaks Park next door.

AMERICAN SWEDISH
INSTITUTE

If lutefisk (item #70) doesn't make you Scandinavian enough, head to the American Swedish Institute in Minneapolis. There's old and new there, and you don't have to be Swedish to appreciate it.

The old is the 1908 Turnblad Mansion, an impressively ornate home along a stretch of Park Avenue once known as the city's "Golden Mile" for its abundance of mansions. The Turnblads lived there briefly before the house became the American Swedish Institute in 1929. The rooms showcase ever-changing exhibits on the culture and traditions of all things Sweden, but the house is its own attraction. Find all eleven porcelain tile stoves (a.k.a., fireplaces), and don't miss the Visby window, an impressive stained glass image that highlights your trip up the grand staircase. And imagine hosting your own party in the second floor ballroom, complete with a stage and skylight.

As for the new, the swanky Nelson Cultural Center houses Fika, a highly regarded restaurant that serves all your favorite Swedish fare. No, the Swedish chef doesn't work there, but the ASI is fit for a king. Sweden's King Carl Gustav visited in 2012.

American Swedish Institute, 2600 Park Ave. S., Minneapolis
612-871-4907, www.asimn.org

SEE THE DRAGON BOAT RACES
ON LAKE PHALEN

A hallmark of the two-day Dragon Festival in St. Paul each summer is the dragon boat races on Lake Phalen. An homage to an ancient Chinese tradition, the impressive forty-foot boats have exquisitely carved and colorful dragon heads and tails at each end. Each boat seats twenty—eighteen paddlers, a drummer, and a flag catcher. The drummer sets a rhythm for the paddlers.

The flag catcher lies belly down on top of the dragon head at the front of the boat and eternally reaches for the flag at the end of the sprint. The first team to catch the flag wins that heat, and several rounds of elimination ensue over the two-day regatta.

Once you've seen the races in person, consider joining a team next year! And don't just come for the races. The entire festival is a showcase of traditional dance and music that will brighten your summer.

Dragon Boat Races, Dragon Festival, Lake Phalen, St. Paul
www.dragonfestival.org

CAPONI ART PARK

It's a special treat to find diamonds among the strip malls and copy-and-paste subdivisions of the suburbs. One such gem is a 60-acre park in Eagen called Caponi Art Park.

Named for its founder, the late artist Anthony Caponi, the park is an eclectic mix of the Caponis' actual backyard (his wife Cheryl still lives on the property); a hidden woods with hiking trails to get away from it all; a series of Caponi-made outdoor sculptures to add to the art of nature; an ampitheater in the woods to enjoy performances; and a scenic overlook with views of both Twin City downtowns.

Open seasonally from May through October, the art park is a free getaway (donations encouraged) from the hustle of the cities and burbs. It's also one of those rare occasions when one man turned over his land to the masses in a space both artists and naturalists will treasure.

Caponi Art Park, 1220 Diffley Road, Eagan
651-454-9412, www.caponiartpark.org

NOTE

Unlike the ever-changing Franconia Scuplture Garden (item #24) or the compact, urban Minneapolis Scuplture Garden (#72), the art pieces at Caponi are more subtle and weaved into a landscape of a heavily wooded terrain. It's almost like nature made the sculptures and placed them right next to that tree.

Be aware, the entrance on Diffley Road sneaks up on you. Slow down!

TOUR
ST. PAUL'S CAVES

St. Paul's riverfront is lined with towering bluffs that offer great views of downtown when you stand on top of them. But what if you stood *inside* the bluffs? There's a network of caves in St. Paul from the days when the bluffs' limestone was mined. Most caves are off-limits for safety reasons, but there's at least one place where you can take a safe tour to get a taste of cave life in St. Paul.

Head over to Wabasha Street Caves on St. Paul's West Side. The building there is built into the bluff and has weekend tours. That's where you'll learn that in addition to mining these caves were once used to grow mushrooms, store cheese, and help brewers. And St. Paul also has a notorious gangster history; some of these caves doubled as speakeasies.

Wabash Street Caves, 215 Wabasha St. S., St. Paul
651-224-1191, www.wabashastreetcaves.com

THE ST. PAUL
MUSEUM TOUR

Downtown St. Paul includes three impressive and family-friendly museums. The Minnesota History Center, Minnesota Children's Museum, and the Science Museum of Minnesota are a few blocks' walk from each other. We've grouped them in this book for those ambitious souls that might want to try all three in a day, but it's fine if you want to slow things down a bit and give them all their due.

Minnesota History Center, 345 Kellogg Blvd. W., St. Paul
651-201-6000, www.minnesotahistorycenter.org

Minnesota Children's Museum, 10 W. Seventh St., St. Paul
651-225-6000, www.mcm.org

Science Museum of Minnesota, 120 W. Kellogg Blvd., St. Paul
651-221-9444, www.smm.org

MINNESOTA HISTORY CENTER

From a history of toys (!), to a look at 1960s Minnesota, to a forty-year retrospective of our vibrant Hmong community, the Minnesota History Center is your go-to place to learn all things Minnesota. Very family friendly with two great stores offering Minnesota wares, the museum has temporary exhibits and permanent displays, such as an interactive look at a Minnesotan's favorite topic: weather. Also check out the moving re-creation of a World War II combat flight inside a military plane in the Minnesota's Greatest Generation area.

And if you go on a Tuesday afternoon in July or August, bring a picnic and stay for an outdoor evening concert.

Minnesota History Center, 345 Kellogg Blvd. W., St. Paul
651-201-6000, www.minnesotahistorycenter.org

MINNESOTA CHILDREN'S MUSEUM

Your only mission at the Minnesota Children's Museum is to play yourself into an impressive nap time. The multifloor spread in downtown St. Paul wants you (and your children, we suppose) to learn by way of playing. The youngest toddlers can crawl around the Habitot, while older kids can act out the things adults do, like shop for groceries or be a postman in the Our World room. And don't miss the rooftop during warm months, where an art world of sand, streams, and tree forts await!

Minnesota Children's Museum, 10 W. Seventh St., St. Paul
651-225-6000, www.mcm.org

NOTE
The museum is open during an expansion project in 2016 and 2017 but there's also a temporary, additional "pop-up" museum in the Mall of America (Item #99) to be open during construction.

SCIENCE MUSEUM OF MINNESOTA

A hands-on, family-friendly explosion of science, you'll go from dinosaur bones and an Egyptian Mummy to learning about the human body by looking at your own cells under a microscope, topped by learning something big in an omnitheater screening. You can also learn about the Mississippi River either from a museum's exhibit, by stopping by the National Park Service's river visitor center, or by looking out the back window, where the river flows by. Make up a song on the musical stairs and, in the summer, learn about rivers and erosion as you play a round of mini golf in the Big Yard.

Science Museum of Minnesota, 120 W. Kellogg Blvd., St. Paul
651-221-9444, www.smm.org

PRO TIP
Sign the family up for an overnight camp-in
at the museum. Sleep near dinosaurs!

JAMES J. HILL HOUSE

When it was completed in 1891, the James J. Hill House was the largest home in Minnesota. It had thirteen bathrooms, twenty-two fireplaces, sixteen chandeliers, and a two-story art gallery—but who's counting? This was a man who could afford to live in luxury. James J. Hill was a railroad baron forever tied to the Great Northern Railway and known in his day as "the Empire Builder" (and a mansion builder, apparently).

This monument to the Gilded Age passed from the Hill family to the Catholic Church for fifty years before the Minnesota Historical Society bought it. Keep in mind that it's a 36,000-square-foot house. The guided tours last seventy-five minutes. So much to see! You can also visit the art gallery without being on the tour.

James J. Hill House, 240 Summit Ave., St. Paul
651-297-2555, www.sites.mnhs.org/historic-sites/james-j-hill-house/

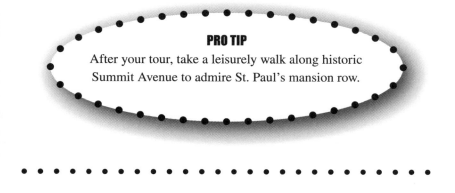

PRO TIP
After your tour, take a leisurely walk along historic Summit Avenue to admire St. Paul's mansion row.

TAKE MOVIE-WATCHING
TO NEW HEIGHTS

You get a sense of what a big deal going to the movies used to be when you head to Heights Theater in suburban Columbia Heights. Built in 1926, the theater was restored in the late 1990s after falling into disrepair. It now screens both first-run and classic films.

It's hard to concentrate on the movies, what with those gorgeous chandeliers to look at—or perhaps the Wurlitzer pipe organ that is played before screenings. Another piano is in the lobby for good measure. Step back into another age, and appreciate the glory of a great historic theater.

Heights Theater, 3951 Central Ave. NE, Columbia Heights
763-789-4992, www.heightstheater.com

CRAWL
AND WHIRL

Two more musts in your art endeavoring in the Twin Cities are the St. Paul Art Crawl in Lowertown and Art-A-Whirl in northeast Minneapolis. Both aim to showcase a lot of art in a concentrated area.

In St. Paul, the Lowertown area has been an artist's haven even when the neighborhood was in the dumps. The Art Crawl dates back to the '70s and now features hundreds of artists showcasing their work to tens of thousands of visitors over a weekend. Take the Green Line LRT there, and spend the day walking amidst the art.

Organizers of Art-A-Whirl proclaim their event the largest open studio tour in the country. With the abundance of old factory space that's been made into art studios, northeast Minneapolis is another artists' haven. And this weekend event, usually in May, invites thousands of people to studios, galleries, and storefronts.

There's a lot of art to be seen at both of these events; you'll appreciate the Twin Cities art scene so much more after attending both.

St. Paul Art Crawl, Lowertown, St. Paul
www.stpaulartcrawl.org/Art-A-Whirl

Northeast Minneapolis
www.nemaa.org/art-a-whirl

SHOPPING AND FASHION

FARMERS MARKETS

Minnesota's shorter growing season is not a barrier to a robust number of Farmers markets that have exploded in number in recent years. So grab your canvas bag and plan a weekend morning at a Farmers market to fully stock your pantry and meet the farmers who grew your grub. The Minneapolis Farmers Market is a large gathering of vendors wedged in next to a highway and a Catholic Basilica. You'll find produce, flowers, crafts, and baked goods. Even live music! The St. Paul Farmers market next to the new St. Paul Saints ballpark in Lowertown is another must, as are several Twin Cities neighborhoods that have their own smaller markets. And there are several winter markets too.

Minneapolis Farmers Market, 312 E. Lyndale Ave. N., Minneapolis
612-333-1718, www.mplsfarmersmarket.com

St. Paul Farmers Market, 290 5th St. E., St. Paul
651-227-8101, www.stpaulfarmersmarket.com

A grassroots effort to track all the Farmers markets around
www.twincitiesfarmersmarkets.com/the-markets/

PICK AND EAT
THE BEST-TASTING APPLES IN THE WORLD

What a wholesome idea: put your family in the minivan and spend an afternoon picking apples that you spend the next month concocting into all assortments of apple-themed entrees, pies, and fritters. But this isn't just a piece of Americana—this is a hearty hat tip to Minnesota, a state rich in apple tradition.

Not only do the state's apple farmers produce millions of apples a year, some of the most beloved apple varieties were developed in the labs of the University of Minnesota, including Honeycrisp and SweeTango. Apples grow really well in Minnesota, so embrace that, gather the kids, and spend a late summer or fall weekend in an orchard, picking your apple bounty.

Directory of Apple Orchards, via Minnesota Dept. of Agriculture
www.mda.state.mn.us/food/minnesotagrown/minnesotaapples.aspx

GO GLOBAL

Visit Mexico, East Africa, Vietnam, and the Middle East at once at the Midtown Global Market at Lake & Chicago in Minneapolis. Housed on the first floor of a repurposed former Sears office building, the market draws shoppers aplenty seeking to catch a meal or stock up for their own pantries.

The Twin Cities has a great assortment of foods from all corners of the earth, but few places feature so many corners in one place. Just strolling through the market is worth it for the pleasant smells.

Both markets and counter-service stores are assembled in one area. Falafel, pasta, and bubble tea for lunch with a locally made draft beer to chase? Sure! Why not? Then stop by the non-food stores to see clothing, crafts, and jewelry from across the globe.

Midtown Global Market, 920 E. Lake St., Minneapolis
612-872-4040, www.midtownglobalmarket.org

GET YOUR SHOPPING FIX
AT 50TH & FRANCE

Whether you're behind on holiday shopping or just want to pamper yourself, you'll find a lot of what you need at the shopping district in Edina known as 50th and France. It's located in and around the intersection of . . . wait for it . . . 50th Street & France Avenue.

More than a hundred shops, boutiques, and restaurants line the streets and nooks in this pedestrian-friendly area not to mention the spas and salons. Several stores cater to brides to be too. And if your companion is way more into shopping than you are, no worries. Head over to the Edina Theater and take in an indie film.

Be sure to come back in the summer when the Edina Art Fair lines the streets.

50th & France, Edina
www.50thandfrance.com/home

FIND STUFF YOU NEVER KNEW YOU NEEDED
AT AX-MAN

For more than fifty years, Ax-Man Surplus has been a must to explore the limits of what can be bought and sold in the commercial market. Need a four-foot red rubber band? Or a beer visor? Or just a huge bag of beads or an inflatable pencil? Ax-Man might have it today, though not necessarily tomorrow.

As they note on their website, Ax-Man "might not have what you need, but we have what you want." Any amount of industrial or electronic surplus or just the stuff in your grandfather's basement is all fair game to be bought and sold. Ax-Man has four locations: St. Paul, St. Louis Park, Fridley, and Crystal.

Ax-Man Surplus
651-646-8653, www.ax-man.com

TAKE
TO THE OPEN STREETS!

Both Minneapolis and St. Paul have experimented with making streets just a little less about cars, which has included changes like bike lanes but also wholesale, daylong closures of long stretches of busy streets to all vehicles.

The series is called Open Streets; both cities have their own take. They're different from festivals and other concert-like events that *happen to require* street closures because, with Open Streets, the act of closing the street *is* the focus. Bike, skate, or just walk about to be more in touch with your neighborhood. It's really about mingling as much as anything.

Major thoroughfares, such as Lyndale, Franklin, Lowry in Minneapolis, and University in St. Paul, have come in for closure during these events. Grab your bike helmet or walking shoes and close the street! Or rather, open it . . . to you!

Open Streets Mpls
www.openstreetsmpls.com

St. Paul Open Streets
www.stpaulopenstreets.org

[ROLLER] COAST
AT THE MALL OF AMERICA

The gargantuan Mall of America is a collection of shopping and superlatives. One of the largest tourist attractions in the world with forty million annual visitors, just to start. But as plentiful as the more than five hundred twenty stores (with no sales tax on clothes in Minnesota) and fifty restaurants are, don't let those be the only reason you go to MOA. Seven acres of floor space in the middle of the mall is the Nickelodeon Universe amusement park. Parents, you'll love having an indoor place to take your kids in the winter. Ride the Log Chute and then giggle afterward at the photos taken of you just before the start of the final drop.

Mall of America, 60 E. Broadway, Bloomington
952-883-8800, www.mallofamerica.com

PRO TIP
The Mall is built on the former Metropolitan Stadium, the Minnesota Twins' first home. Look for home plate, then look along the walls for the one remaining stadium seat that marks where slugger Harmon Killebrew once parked a five hundred twenty-two-foot home run in 1967.

GET A SHAVE, A SHINE,
AND A SHIRT AT HEIMIE'S

You can't help but feel treated like royalty when you step into Heimie's Haberdashery in downtown St. Paul. Descendants of the original Heimie's Menswear that opened in the 1910s operate this updated version of full-service store with an old-school feel. Suits, shirts, and trousers are made to order, but stop by for a shoeshine and a trim at the barbershop. Let the haberdashers at Heimie's walk you through the process of learning what it takes to know your shirts. There's pretty much a 100% guarantee you'll look even better when you leave.

Heimie's Haberdashery, 400 St. Peter St., St. Paul
651-224-2354, www.heimies.com

SUGGESTED ITINERARIES

DOWNTOWN MINNEAPOLIS RIVERFRONT

DOWNTOWN ST. PAUL

IN AND AROUND THE UNIVERSITY OF MINNESOTA

DEFEAT WINTER

REALLY JUST TOO COLD? TRY THESE INDOOR WINTER ACTIVITIES

A COZY SUMMER EVENING OUTDOORS

STATE FAIR

• •

FESTIVALS
BY SEASON

SPRING

Art-A-Whirl & St. Paul Art Crawl, 117
Cinco de Mayo West Side Celebration, 48
Minneapolis-St. Paul International Film Festival, 18

SUMMER

Bike tours—St. Paul Classic & Minneapolis Bike Tour, 54
Dragon Boat Races, Lake Phalen, 107
Grand Old Day, 27
Hmong Freedom Celebration, a.k.a. "J4," 28
Minnesota Fringe Festival, 26
Northern Spark, 44

AUTUMN

Halloween Outdoor Puppet Extravaganza, 32
Minnesota Renaissance Festival, 42

WINTER

ACTIVITIES
BY SEASON

SPRING

Bike Rentals / Nice Ride MN, 50

Do Farm Chores at the Oliver H. Kelley Farm, 81

Franconia Sculpture Park, 33

Historic Fort Snelling, 108

May Day Parade, 36

Minnesota & Como Zoos, 23

SUMMER

Bike Rentals / Nice Ride MN, 50

Bike to Stillwater, 69

Bike Tours—St. Paul Classic & Minneapolis Bike Tour, 54

Defeat of Jesse James Days, 96

Gush Over the Falls—Minnehaha Falls, 52

Minnehaha Creek, 72

Minnesota Fringe Festival, 26

Minnesota State Fair Amateur Talent Contest, 37

Miracle of Birth Center at the Minnesota State Fair, 91

Music & Movies in the Park, 34

AUTUMN

WINTER

INDEX

• •

• •

• •

• •

• •

• •